Survival
Against the Odds

Ian Rohr

sundance™

Published by
Sundance Publishing
33 Boston Post Road West
Suite 440
Marlborough, MA 01752
800-343-8204
www.sundancepub.com

First published 2002 by
Blake Education, Locked Bag 2022, Glebe 2037, Australia
Exclusive United States Distribution: Sundance Publishing

Design by Cliff Watt in association with
Sundance Publishing

Survival Against the Odds
ISBN 978-0-7608-6698-6

Photo Credits:
p. 8 Rodney Fox Shark Expedition-www.rodneyfox.com.au; p. 9
photolibrary.com; p. 11 Rodney Fox Shark Expedition-www.rodneyfox.com.au;
p. 15 (top) APL/Corbis, (bottom right) APL/Corbis; p. 17 (top) APL/Corbis,
(bottom) Image courtesy of Circus World Museum, Baraboo, Wisconsin with
permission from Ringling Bros and Barnum and Bailey; pp. 18–19 APL/Corbis;
p. 21 (bottom) Associated Press, London; pp. 24–29 NASA.

Printed by Nordica International Ltd.
Manufactured in Guangzhou, China
March, 2019
Nordica Job#: CA21900406
Sundance/Newbridge PO#: 229269

Table of Contents

Must stay calm.

Close Encounters of the Wild Kind

Warning! You never know what is lurking behind the next tree or beneath the next wave.

Most wild animals want to stay well away from us, perhaps sensing that people are the deadliest animals of all. But sometimes they do attack. If that happens, survival can be a matter of staying calm, thinking quickly . . . and having a lot of luck.

If you do have a close encounter with a wild animal, it always pays to keep your head. Staying calm can mean you live to tell the story.

A Grizzly Moment

The best way to avoid trouble with bears is to stay away from them. But sometimes, even the experts get into trouble.

This Is Not a Bluff!

Keeping her head helped to save Barbara Moore's life. Barbara, a national park ranger, was walking in bear country in Yellowstone National Park when she came across a dead bison. She suspected that a bear had killed it. And she knew it was dangerous to come between a bear and its dinner. Then, she saw a huge grizzly bear charging at her. Most bear charges are a **bluff**, so Barbara stood still. But this charge was no bluff. The bear knocked her to the ground.

Playing Dead

Barbara's heart raced as the bear clawed her. She curled up and pretended to be dead. The bear rolled her over three times. At last, the bear wandered away with its cubs. Barbara had convinced the grizzly that she was no threat.

Yellowstone National Park

Mother bears with cubs account for more than 80 percent of bear attacks.

If a grizzly bear gets down on all fours and lays its ears back, get ready for the charge.

This will make a lovely rug for my den.

?!

SURVIVAL TIPS: GRIZZLY BEAR ATTACK

Grizzly bears are brown bears. Brown bears attack if they feel their cubs, their territory, or their dinner is in danger. Playing dead can be a good tactic. But it takes courage to lie still while a wild animal gives you the once-over.

Method 1 Lie face down flat on the ground. Lock your fingers behind your head, with your arms protecting the sides of your head.

Method 2 Lie on your side curled into a ball. Bury your head into your knees. Wrap your arms around your legs and lock your wrists together.

Don't play dead if you happen to meet a black bear. They eat dead things!

Hunter or Hunted?

Imagine being attacked by a great white shark and living to tell about it. Would you then go back into shark-infested waters to teach others to understand the creature that nearly killed you?

Rodney Fox before the attack. His wet suit would later help to hold his torn body together until he reached the hospital.

Fishing for Danger

Rodney Fox was a champion at his favorite sport, spear-fishing. But one day the hunter became the hunted. As Rodney took aim with his speargun, a great white shark hit him from behind. The force of the attack knocked the speargun from his hand and the mask off his face. The shark's jaws clamped around his back.

He clawed at the shark's eyes. It released its grip. He wrapped his body around the shark so it couldn't get at him. But he needed air—badly. He let go and floated to the surface. Looking down through the bloody sea, he saw open jaws and teeth coming at him again. He tried to kick them away.

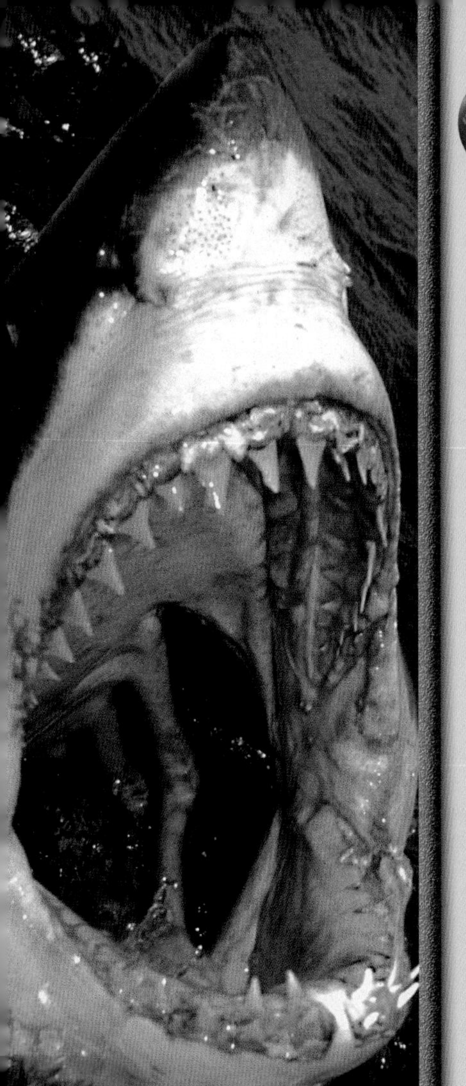

A great white shark's jaws push right out of its mouth, so the shark hits its prey teeth first.

How Many Teeth Does a Shark Have?

Sharks never run out of brand-new teeth ready for action. Their teeth grow in rows, which move slowly forward. When a front tooth snaps off, a new one from the next row swings in to fill the gap. This happens about every two weeks. A shark may go through as many as 20,000 teeth in its lifetime!

Vital Statistics

Name: GREAT WHITE SHARK
Length: 4.3 to 4.6 meters (14 to 15 ft)
Weight: 520 to 770 kg (1,000 to 1,700 lbs)
Open jaws: over 1 meter (3 ft) wide
Teeth: 4 cm (1.5 in.) long, **serrated** like the blade on a steak knife

Alive!

Suddenly, the shark turned and grabbed the fish on Rodney's belt rope. It pulled the fish—and Rodney—down. Then, the rope snapped. Rodney made it back to the surface and was quickly pulled into a boat. He was barely alive.

Some of the stitches on Rodney's upper body. He didn't want to be pulled from the water by his damaged arms. He was afraid that they would come off.

As Rodney was lifted from the boat to a waiting car, his side gaped open, and coils of his **intestines** slid out. A friend pushed them back in. Then the car sped off to the hospital, 65 kilometers (40 miles) away.

Survival Tips: Shark Attack

Sharks are **predators**. They will usually only attack if they think they can win. So, you have more chance of surviving an attack if you let the shark know that you are not defenseless. The parts of a shark's body most sensitive to pain are its eyes and gills. Hit the gills or eyes with your fist, camera, or anything else you have.

Make quick, sharp jabs at the eyes or gills.

The nose is not as sensitive to pain. Only hit here if you cannot reach the eyes or gills.

Killer to Keeper

Rodney needed hundreds of stitches—465 on his upper body alone. His left lung had been punctured, and his **spleen** and a major **artery** were exposed. But he shocked everyone by surviving.

Rodney was nervous about going back into the sea. When he did, he killed many sharks. Then he realized that fear was not a good reason to kill. He set out to learn more about sharks and their behavior. Today, he **campaigns** to save the animals that nearly took his life.

With underwater cameraman Ron Taylor, Rodney later made the first film of great white sharks.

Phew! Escaped just in time . . .

Violent Forces

Few things in nature could be more threatening than a rumbling volcano.

Violent forces shaped our planet. And these forces haven't finished yet. Sometimes, with little or no warning, fiery rock can blast from volcanoes, and rivers of **lava** can start to flow. Or more deadly eruptions can fill the air with poisonous gases and dust that burn and destroy everything in their path.

Every year, about 60 volcanoes around the world erupt. Most of these eruptions cause little damage. But some claim thousands of lives. There are also some amazing escape stories. How did those people survive the odds?

Eruption!

The town leaders had said there was nothing to worry about—Mount Pelée was completely safe.

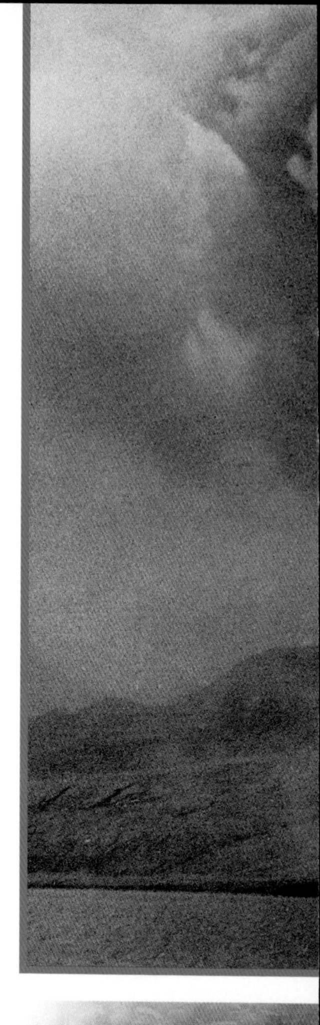

The Election That Wiped Out a Town

It was April 1902. The gray sky above St. Pierre on the island of Martinique was filled with ash. The air smelled of **sulfur**, and snakes and spiders from Mount Pelée invaded the town!
But the government did not want to **evacuate** the town until after the election, set for May 10. They even sent out troops to stop people from leaving.

Then, at about 7:50 AM on May 8, 1902, the top of Mount Pelée exploded. A burning cloud of gas and dust ran down the mountainside at speeds up to 161 kilometers per hour (100 mph). This glowing cloud was a scorching 700° Celsius (about 1,300° F). At 8:03 AM, a ship in the harbor sent the message, "St. Pierre destroyed by Pelée eruption." Over 29,000 people were dead. But two people had survived.

Before the eruption, 50 people and 200 animals died of snakebite in one day.

Huge clouds of ash pour from Mount Pelée. A crewman on a ship in the harbor saw people "running . . . amidst the flames until a terrible cloud . . . came, when they fell like flies."

Today, Mount Pelée still stands behind the rebuilt town of St. Pierre.

The Survivors

Auguste Cyparis was in jail, in an underground cell. There was one small, grated opening cut into the wall above the door. And the door faced away from the volcano. Cyparis was waiting for his breakfast when a dark cloud filled his cell. He held his breath as hot air and ash rushed through the grate. He was badly burned and in great pain, but he survived four days in the ruins before being rescued.

Léon Comprère-Léandre was a young shoemaker who lived on the edge of town. He was sitting on his doorstep when the burning cloud hit. He made it inside, his arms, legs, and body burning. Léon threw himself on his bed to die. Then he came to and saw the roof was on fire. His legs bleeding and covered with burns, he somehow found the strength to run six kilometers (four miles) to the next town.

Types of Volcanic Eruptions

Not all volcanic eruptions are the same. Sometimes a small opening only oozes a trickle of lava. Other times the force of a blast can explode the side of the mountain. What comes out of a volcano is also not always the same. It could be

- an eruption cloud of ash and gas.
- lava.
- pieces of rock, ash, and dust called pyroclastics. (Pyroclastic flows, full of burning gas, are much more deadly than lava flows. Today we know that the Mount Pelée eruption was a pyroclastic flow.)
- poisonous gases.

NOTE: If you think or are told that a volcano is going to blow, get out of town!

The ruins of St. Pierre. Most people died within seconds of breathing in the dust and burning gas.

Cyparis survived to tour the world in a circus act, under the name Ludger Sylbaris.

Inside a Volcano

Surviving a helicopter crash is amazing enough. Three men then had to survive the crash site—the inside of an active volcano!

Talk About a Hot Spot

In 1992, cameramen Michael Benson and Chris Duddy were sent to Hawaii to film a smoking volcano for the movie *Sliver*. They hired helicopter pilot Craig Hosking and flew over Pu'u O'o **crater** on Kilauea Volcano. Filming was not going well. It was almost impossible to see the crater. It was covered in choking gases coming from the pools of lava and **vents**.

The helicopter engine began to splutter. Hosking fought the controls. But the helicopter headed straight over the rim of the smoking crater.

It just missed the pool of glowing lava, crashing on a rock ledge. All three men managed to scramble from the wreckage.

Now they were stranded 50 meters (164 ft) below the crater's rim. They were breathing in choking fumes and were deafened by the roar in the crater. They could feel the heat of the bubbling lava through their boots.

What Is an Active Volcano?

Scientists put volcanoes into three groups.

1. An *active volcano* is one that has erupted within the last few hundred years. It may or may not currently be erupting, but it is likely to at some stage in the future.
2. A *dormant volcano* has not erupted in the last few hundred years, but it has erupted during the last several thousand years.
3. An *extinct volcano* has not erupted during the last several thousand years. But that is no guarantee that it won't erupt again!

Kilauea holds the record for the longest continuous eruption in the twentieth century. It has been erupting since 1983.

Out On a Ledge

The three men tried to climb the crumbling slope and reach clearer air. But they kept slipping up to their knees in hot, black soot. Hosking wrapped his shirt around his face and returned to the wreck to try to fix the radio. Success! He managed to guide a rescue helicopter to his location and leap inside. Hosking was flown to safety. The pilot couldn't reach the other two men, however, because the heat and gas had damaged the helicopter.

Day 1: *Hosking rescued near crashed helicopter*

Day 2: *Duddy manages to climb out*

Day 3: *Benson rescued from inside crater*

Pu'u O'o crater was about 300 m (1,000 ft) across. Bad weather and thick clouds of gas made it impossible for rescuers to see inside. They tried to drop packages of food and water to Benson. All he saw was a shape dropping through the thick fumes. Benson thought it was Duddy falling to his death.

Two To Go

Benson and Duddy spent the night in the choking fumes inside the crater. The next day, Duddy decided to try the dangerous climb again. This time he made it to the top where he was rescued by park rangers. Benson was not such a good climber. He spent another night in the hot gases and freezing rain. Finally, at first light on day three, a second rescue helicopter flew over the rim of the crater. The pilot let a large net dangle where he guessed Benson might be. On the third drop, he guessed right. Benson saw his only chance, grabbed the net, and was pulled to safety.

Some Hawaiians believe that a powerful and fiery goddess, Pele, lives in Kilauea volcano.

Overhanging rim

Helicopter wreckage

Lava pool

Michael Benson after his rescue. He suffered serious lung damage.

Ehh, we should have turned right at the Moon . . .

At Risk in Space

"Okay, Houston, we've had a problem here."

When the crew of *Apollo 13* radioed those historic words, they were more than 330,000 kilometers (about 205,000 miles) away from home. And the problem was a serious one.

What began as a voyage to the Moon soon turned into a life-threatening ordeal for the three astronauts aboard. They knew that the odds of returning safely to Earth were slim. In fact, there was a good chance they would spend their last hours spinning around between Earth and the Moon.

Destination: Moon

Do you believe that 13 is an unlucky number? *Apollo 13* blasted off at 13 minutes past 2:00 PM on April 11, 1970. And from the start, it was a very unlucky voyage.

The Journey Begins

It was to be the third landing on the Moon for the United States. By April 13, the astronauts had settled into their long journey. Then, a sudden loud explosion filled the silence of space. A high-pitched alarm sounded in the Command Module, and warning lights flashed on the control panels.

Apollo 13 rockets into space with the help of a huge *Saturn V* rocket.

The astronauts quickly checked everything. They discovered that an oxygen tank, part of *Apollo 13*'s fuel system, had exploded in the Service Module. The explosion had also made a hole in the side of the spacecraft. But the astronauts did not realize this right away. Then Commander Jim Lovell saw a cloud of white oxygen floating past the window. They realized then that they were in big trouble.

Jack Swigert

APOLLO 13: CREW PROFILES

Name	**Job**	**Particulars**
Jim Lovell	Commander	Experienced. This was his second trip to the Moon
Fred Haise	Lunar Module pilot	Knew his spacecraft inside out.
Thomas Mattingly	Command Module pilot	He was exposed to German measles and had to be replaced.
Jack Swigert	Command Module pilot	Replaced Mattingly. An expert on what to do in an emergency.

Jim Lovell

Thomas Mattingly

Fred Haise

The official crew portrait taken during training for the mission.

Floating in a Tin Can

The astronauts were more than three and a half days from returning to Earth. But the Command Module's power and oxygen supplies would now last only a few hours.

Locked in Space

The crew moved from the crippled Command Module to the Lunar Module. This was designed to keep two men alive for two days. Now it would have to **sustain** three men for about four days. They had to reserve vital supplies of power and cooling water for the spacecraft. So the men sat in freezing temperatures and drank only small amounts of water.

An entire panel of the Service Module was blown away when the oxygen tank exploded.

***Apollo 13* was made up of three connecting sections.**

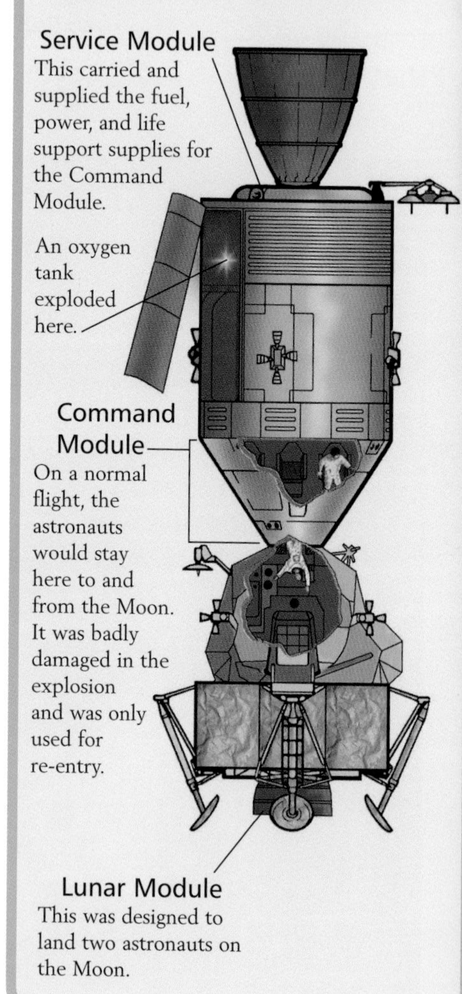

Mission Control in Houston, Texas

New Instructions

As they swung around the Moon, the crew corrected their position to put them on course for home, three days away. They knew that the Command Module's engines would not have enough power to position them for re-entry into the Earth's **atmosphere**. The Lunar Module was not designed to do it—but it was their only chance. Mission Control would have to quickly calculate hundreds of new instructions and relay them to the crew.

Why Is Re-Entry Dangerous?

Re-entry into the Earth's atmosphere is one of the most dangerous parts of space travel. If the spacecraft comes in too steep, it'll burn up like a meteorite. If it comes in too shallow, it'll bounce back into space. And the crew is totally on its own. Blazing hot air around the spacecraft makes it impossible to receive or send radio transmissions.

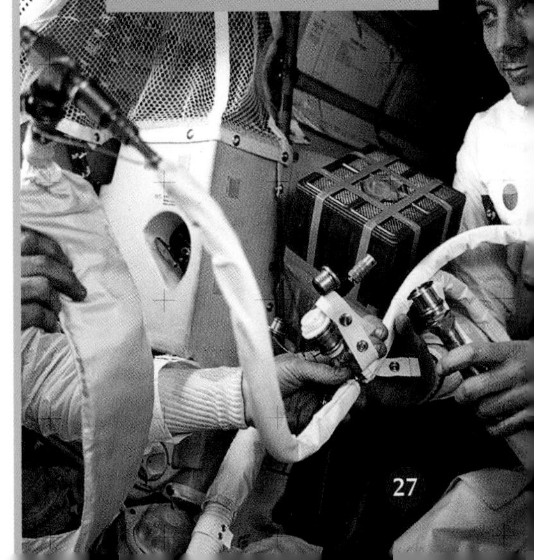
The crew also faced the risk of carbon dioxide poisoning, so they made their own air filter.

Jack Swigert is lifted aboard a helicopter in a rescue net. Amazingly, *Apollo 13* landed closer to the intended pick-up point than any other Apollo mission.

Homeward Bound

There were no fax machines on the spacecraft of the 1970s, so the astronauts had to copy down two hours of instructions. One error could cause disaster and death. As re-entry drew closer, the men moved back to the Command Module. Empty for four days, it was icy cold, and moisture covered the instruments.

After splashdown and helicopter recovery, the crew of the *Apollo 13* mission step aboard the recovery ship.

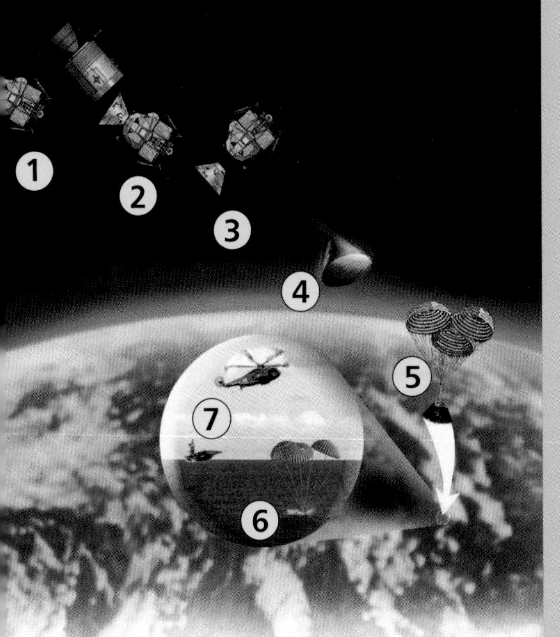

***Apollo 13*'s Re-Entry**

1 The astronauts use the engines of the Lunar Module to position *Apollo 13* for re-entry.
2 They release the Service Module.
3 They release the Lunar Module.
4 Re-entry—the Command Module hits the Earth's atmosphere. All communication is lost for four minutes.
5 The astronauts are okay. Parachutes on the Command Module open to slow down its speed for landing.
6 *Apollo 13* splashes into the Pacific Ocean only 5.5 km (3.5 miles) from the rescue ship.
7 The crew is rescued by helicopter and ship.

The tired men repositioned the Lunar Module's engines, using the new instructions. If the electronics were wet, they could **malfunction**. And if things didn't work the first time, it was unlikely there would be power for a second chance. Once in position, the crew **jettisoned** the Service Module. Next, the Lunar Module was released, and the men watched it drift off into space.

Hundreds of people at Mission Control worked around the clock to get the astronauts home.

Then, strapped in their seats in the Command Module, the men hurtled toward home. Radio contact was lost during re-entry, and a tense four minutes passed before Lovell's voice came over the Mission Control speakers. He said one word.

"Okay."

Make a Shelter

If your life takes a turn toward disaster, knowing how to find shelter might just help you to survive!

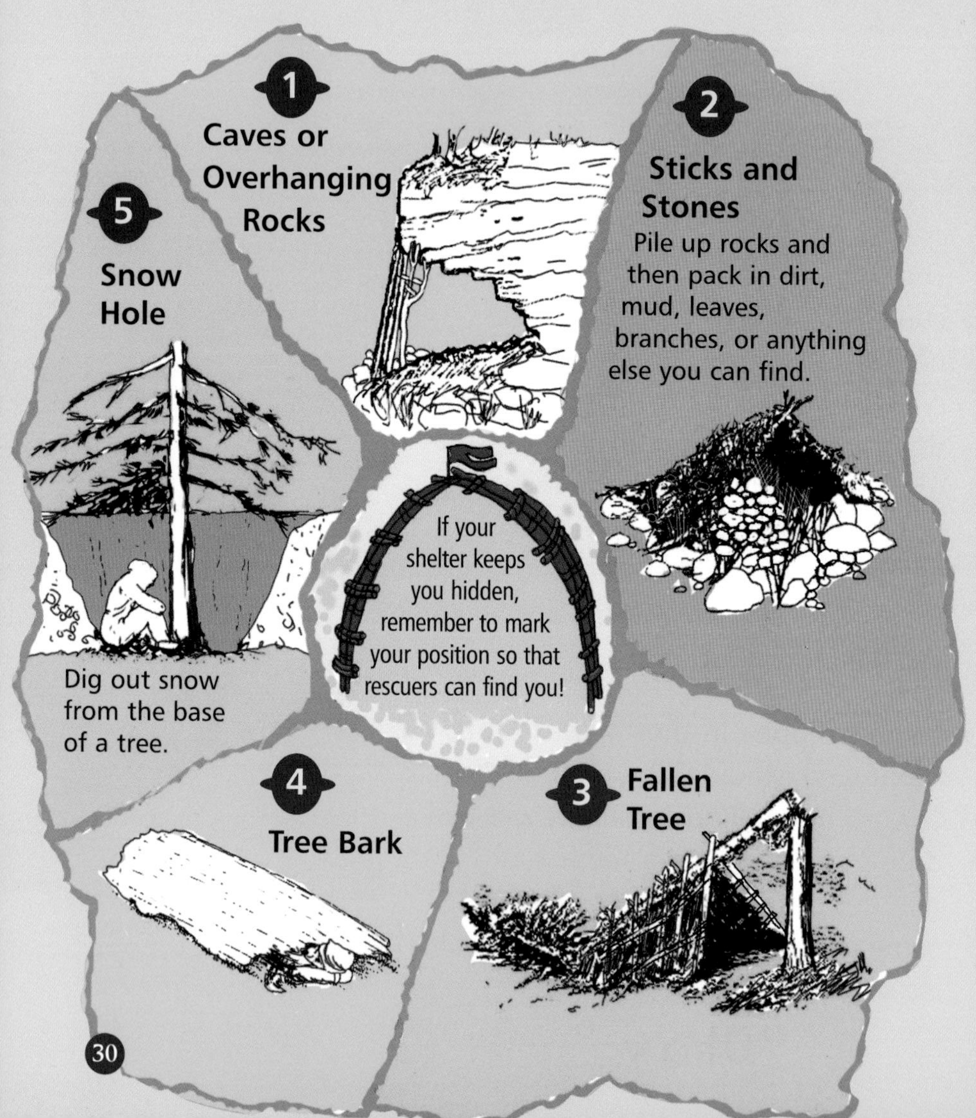

Glossary

artery vessels that transport blood from the heart to the rest of the body

atmosphere the gasses surrounding the Earth

bluff to gain an advantage by pretending to be stronger

campaigns efforts to change or to bring attention to an issue

crater the widened top of a volcano vent

evacuate to move from an area threatened by disaster

intestines the tubular part of the digestive system

jettisoned objects thrown away or dropped to lighten a ship's or aircraft's load

lava magma (hot liquid rock and gases) that has erupted from a volcano

malfunction to fail to work properly

predators animals that hunt other animals

serrated having sharp notches along the edge

spleen a human organ that removes worn-out blood cells

sulfur an element with a rotten egg smell

sustain to supply with vital needs, such as air, food, and water

vents holes or cracks in Earth's surface that lava flows through

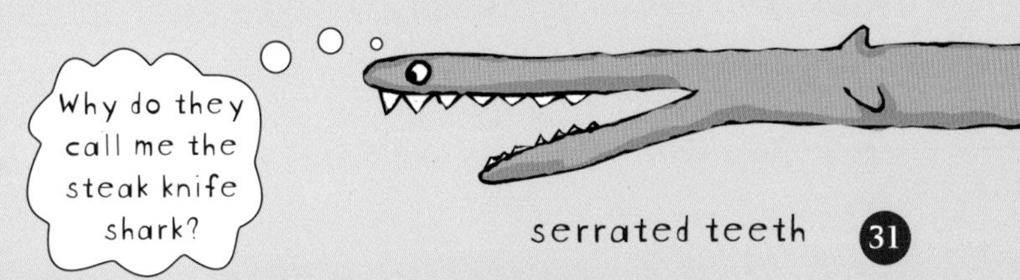

serrated teeth

Index